Withycombe Raleigh

of Yesteryear

Part Two

Sally Stocker • Elizabeth Gardner
Christopher Long • Maurice Southwell

Our families have lived in the village for generations. Working as a team we have combined our own memorabilia with local knowledge. Maurice then put the mass of information and photographs into some kind of order! We enjoyed doing it – we hope you enjoy it as well!

Our grateful thanks to all those kind people, known – particularly Richard Tarr – and unknown, who furnished us with the photographs and information on Withycombe Raleigh, and whose work may be reproduced here.

This book is dedicated to our families – past and present.

GW00501943

OBELISK PUBLICATIONS

We have over 200 Devon titles; for a current list please send an SAE to
Obelisk Publications, 2 Church Hill, Pinhoe, Exeter EX4 9ER. Tel: 01392 468556

First published in 2005 by
Obelisk Publications, 2 Church Hill, Pinhoe, Exeter, Devon
Designed by Chips and Sally Barber
Typeset by Sally Barber
Printed in Great Britain
by Avocet Press, Cullompton, Devon

©2005 Obelisk Publications

Withycombe Raleigh

of Yesteryear

Part Two

As its name suggests, this book is the second part of a 'journey' through Withycombe Raleigh by means of old postcards and photographs combined with the memories of some enthusiastic 'locals'. Part Two generally contains more up-to-date images, and continues to tell the story of this ancient village, which, although enveloped by greater Exmouth, retains its village feel and still boasts many long-established families.

We start with two views of Phear Park. These historic wrought iron gates at the entrance were 'missing' for over fifty years. They were eventually tracked down by Lionel Howell, Chairman of the 531st Tribute Fund, who found them at the site of the old Exmouth Water Works in Hamilton Lane. Restored to their former glory, they now once more proudly stand welcoming people into Phear Park. The photograph below is of the D-Day Wall of Remembrance, which was unveiled and dedicated on 10 June 2001.

The date is 12 April 1953 and the scene is still Phear Park, with the Ian Allan special train approaching Exmouth from the direction of Budleigh Salterton. Ashleigh Road and Phear Avenue can be seen on the right, while, to the left, golfers enjoy a relatively peaceful round.

The van shown to the left belonged to a business that traded from 23 Withycombe Road.

Below, the group assembled in 1958 for a photo was the 299 Air Training Corps, Exmouth; they were visiting RAF Henlow, Bedford. Comprising mainly Exmouth members, but with some from Budleigh Salterton and Sidmouth, their headquarters were in Phear Park. The following people have been recognised: Messrs Shargool, Rendell, Gosling, Rye, Bernard, Salter, Coleman. Robinson, Hoskins, Clarke, McCartney, Wallace, Lunnon, Pope, Partridge, Mather, Donovan, Parker, Donovan, Flying Officer Greenaway, Flight Lieutenant Harding, Squadron Leader Widgly, and Flying Officer Coote.

There was a time when the lower parts of Exmouth and Withycombe were prone to flooding. Here are just two examples. The picture above shows Park Road in flood. You can see the former railway viaduct in the background; the Withycombe Brook is flowing in from the right.

Below, the Withycombe Brook is in full flood. The spot can be readily identified, because the telegraph pole and wall to the left of the picture are still there. However, the picturesque Mill Cottages are no longer with us. They had already been evacuated during the autumn flood in 1960, but rather than fall foul of water, they were consumed by fire, in July 1962, caused by a spark from a bonfire. Ironically, this was on the hottest day of the year and coincided with the auction of the miller's equipment, which was being held in the adjacent Withycombe Mill.

Here we see Mill Cottages in the aftermath of the 1960 flood. The occupants had to be evacuated during the flooding after a large crack appeared, as seen in the picture, running from top to bottom of one gable end of the cottages. The residents were never to return. It must have been a major shock to Mrs Sharland; she had lived there for 63 years.

Below, soldiers are helping to build a sandbag wall, hoping to prevent further flooding by the Withycombe Brook. They also helped with the clear-up in the aftermath of the flood. The school wall and cedar tree are still there, so help to place the scene.

Miller H. J. Long had a vested interest in the level of the waters of the brook, so he kept a record of the floods from 1886 until 1936. The heights were recorded from the mill's floor to the red clay mud marks left on the door at the mill. Here are some of those flood measurements he recorded: 26 December 1886 – 26 inches; 19 November 1894 – 21 inches; 27 October 1903 – 18 inches; 22 December 1909 – 14 inches; 27 October 1929 – 22 inches; 5 December 1929 – 15 inches; 19 January 1935 – 18 inches; 28 May 1936 – 15 inches. The records taken of the flood levels in 1960 were as follows: 30 September – 38 inches; 6 October – 34 inches.

The lovely picture below was taken by photographer Richard Tarr in the summer of 1962. The children, from left to right, were Simon Cordrey and Susan, Christopher, David and Stephen Long. Frank Bastin is standing behind them. Made by the Berry Family of Woodbury, the mill wheel is, sadly, no longer in the village, but is now displayed in a flowerbed at the beginning of the Plantation and Bath Road, Exmouth.

The picture above is of a previous Withycombe Water Mill, circa 1804. The site of this earlier mill is unknown, but was probably near the Phear Park Lodge. By sharp contrast, the scene below made a sad day for the miller's children, as they watched the demolition of the Withycombe (Marpool) Mill to make way for the flood relief channel. For years the picturesque mill was visited and admired by thousands of visitors; it was also the subject of many postcards.

The scenes on the opposite page give an idea of a 'before and after' scenario. At the top is the recently constructed school bridge (February 2003) in Withycombe Village Road. The view below shows how the area would have looked 40 years ago, just after the flood in 1960. The Mill was still operational, and you can see the bank that was constructed as a temporary flood prevention measure.

Withycombe Raleigh of Yesteryear – Part Two

This final flood picture from 1960 was taken in Moorfield Road. The two car drivers were chancing their luck in an attempt to manoeuvre in the swirling waters. Marpool Bakery and the general store of Mr and Mrs R. H. Escott can be seen in the distance.

The small photo to the right is of the Withycombe Parish Church Bell Ringers of 1949. Featured are G. Rendell, C. Deem, J. Deem, W. Hayman, F. Bastin, J. Skinner, W. Clifton, and F. Dymond.

Below are the members of the Withycombe Parish Church Choir enjoying their Christmas party in 1973. Included in this picture are the Revd A. R. and Mrs Leigh.

Above are the members of the Withycombe Parish Church Choir as they looked in 1967. Those present that day included the following: Revd D. A. Lingwood, vicar; Revd I. Gregory, curate; Mr H. G. Taylor, choirmaster; and Mr Geoff Perryman, organist. The identified choir members were Mrs N. West, Mrs Begbie, Miss Taylor, Mrs Lane, D. Wills, P. Shackleford, Tommy Harvey, D. Whitehead, A. Dustan, R. Dustan and Mr Richards.

Below, a coach trip to Dartmoor was the treat which lay in store for these choirboys of 1960. Within their ranks are George Woolacott, Barry Hicks, Nigel Shepherd, Steven Gazzard, Ernest Jarvis, Philip Humphries, Elwyn Bowyer and Dave Butt.

The Council's nursery greenhouses, which produced the bedding plants for all of East Devon's public parks and gardens, were once here in Withycombe. As this sequence shows, they are no longer with us; the area is now occupied by the aptly named Nursery Close and Nursery Mews. Pictured left are nurserymen Stan Evens (left) and Ron Franks. When the nursery closed in 1985, there were two other nurserymen, Chris Long and Derrick Salter. In 1990 the nursery was demolished and work began on Nursery Close.

The picture below shows how the demolition and excavation made it possible to see the Holly Tree Inn from the Moorfield Road site.

There's nothing like a good bonfire! This was the Nursery Close building site in 1990.

And this is what it replaced. Ducks were happily at play in the field at the rear of the old Post Office and Bakery; this is now part of Nursery Close. The cul-de-sac was finished and the first houses were occupied on 2 February 1991.

Marked 'The Holly Tree', 'Claude West', and 'Withycombe', do you know anything of the history behind the objects of local pottery shown here? If you do, we'd like to hear about them.

Happy, smiling faces, and no wonder! Biscuits and 'pop' provided a real treat for this group of youngsters from Park Way. Amongst those enjoying their 1953 Coronation party were Geoff Osborne, Maurice Wood, Dave Hitchcock, Brian Chave, Fred Hitchcock and Peter Chave.

Below, we have the same year and occasion, but a different street. Identified in the scene are Fred Burch, Mrs Tew, Vera, Barbara and Alan, Susan and Marilyn Needs, Roger Gregory, Bobby Dennet, Becky Markham, Mrs Jarvis, Mrs Bowman, Heather Luxton, Marion White, Ian Wilson and Carol Routledge.

Opposite (top), it was a case of 'Ready, steady, go!' for Jill Veness, Joy Elston, Josephine Rowsell and Mary Brownjohn, who were among those who enjoyed their 1953 Coronation party at Green Close.

At the bottom of the page we have moved on twenty years, and here we see the Withycombe Methodist Playschool Christmas Party of 1972. Included in this picture are Barbara England, Saul Goodwin, Darren England, Matthew French, Caleb Goodwin, Michael Slater, Scott Bartlett, Phillip Salter, Tom Page, Damon and Charmaine Hitchcock and Jill and Tamsin French.

The small picture in the middle is of Jack Sharland, proudly displaying his trophy alongside his magnificent carnival entry. The horse brasses belonged to the Burch Family; the two children on the float were Ken and Pat Martin from Park Terrace. Boldbrook and the garden wall of The

Cottage can be recognised in the background of this late 1940s photo.

The map overleaf was surveyed in 1933, but was amended with additions in 1938. The dotted lines, such as Moorfield Road, indicate projects that were planned, but not yet completed. A close examination is recommended; it shows just how much this area has changed, particularly to the north of the 'village'.

Opposite top, several classes combined for this 1953 Coronation photograph at Withycombe Raleigh Primary School. Among those recognised are Terry Hobbs, Jane Strudwick, Ann Clark, Philip Smith, Barbara Tew, Ann Sedgemore, David Hellier, Jane Madge, Mike Sydenham, Angela Reddicliffe, Frances Bartlett, Susan Lucas, Chris Lunn, Maureen Smith, Chris Tate, Eric Evans, Brenda Brain, Pat Bontoff, Susan Needs, Trevor Pike and Rose Cotton.

The middle picture dates back to the late 1940s; within these ranks were Roy Hatton, Ron Lavis, Molly Hall, Dorothy Bamsey, Les Franks and Eileen Grant.

April 1936 saw the opening of the new Garden of Rest for Withycombe. This created a quiet and pleasant retreat. The photo shows a blessing being given by the Lord Bishop of Exeter. In February 1967, the road was widened here. Thought to have been last used a century earlier, a number of lead-lined coffins, in nine brick-built vaults, were uncovered. They contained the remains of twenty Withycombe residents, who were then given a final resting place at St John's in-the-Wilderness.

On a less morbid note, the top picture here shows a convivial evening circa 1950 at the Holly Tree. Present that night were Claude and Lil West, 'Johnny' Dymond, Margaret Boddington, Archie Dymond, Cath Capel, Vic Boddington and Colin Capel.

Below, notice the old gaslight, and look at the silhouette of the cottages behind the Holly Tree – no, not the pub, but the ancient tree that gave it its name. These now overlook the main road; the road widening that took away part of the burial ground also removed Moorfield Dairy and the old Recreation/Reading Room, and thereby removed a traffic bottleneck.

Two coaches and a bus provide a small element of continuity here. The top photo is from 1956 and shows a rugby club outing from the Holly Tree Inn. It includes the following people: Bert Dymond, Mrs Burch, Nibs Burch, Bert Tozer, Rodney Tucker, Roy Hunt, Brian Tozer, Jack Burch, Mr and Mrs Rendall, Geoff Greenaway, Ivan Turner, Fred

Morrish, Gerry Rowland, Jim Stewart, Peggy Lewis, Harry Greenaway, Alf Bowden, Mr Fairchild, Win Stuart, Colin Bright, Jack Franks and Mrs Lane.

The middle outing was from the Country House pub. Devon General's Withycombe Bus, with DDV427 and route 82 on the front, was a familiar sight when we had a regular route through the village. This was the spot where, in about 1944, the wheel of a military vehicle somehow sunk into the road surface and the vehicle partly toppled onto the hedge, setting the gaslight on fire!

Above, we see 'rush hour' in Withycombe, before the road widening in 1966/67.

The photo to the right contains a few more well-known faces from the village: Eileen England, Gladys Willmot and Doris and Joyce Townsend.

Below, Myra Chapman and Hilary Southwell were the two young girls enjoying the fun at a 1950 fête in Raleigh Park.

With so many green fields around, it's not surprising that sport has played a large part in village life. During the Second World War, teams from local schools tested their skills against evacuees from other parts of the country. In this photo, above, from about 1944, Alan Southwell, Harold Gatter, Arthur Hodge, Peter Tanton, Mr Reid, Joe Turner, Ron Worsley, Les Franks, Derek Kettle and Stan Pike were involved in such matches. The Headmaster of the secondary school was Mr Bullied; he is shown here with some of his charges.

Taken about four years later, the picture below is of the Withycombe Rugby Football Club of 1948/49. Those featured include Jack Wilson, Peter Southwell, Jim Stuart, Mervyn Upcot, Geoff Willmot, Geoff McNamara, Fred French, Harry Willmot, Morgan Willmot, Arthur Hellier, Roy Tootell, Alan Young, Maunder, Jeff Barr, Rodney Tucker, Sansom, Peter Mair, Les Franks, Nibs Burch, Fred Burch, Jack Lott and Stuart Fudge.

Withycombe Raleigh of Yesteryear – Part Two

The ball was smaller, red and a different shape for these 1956 members of Withycombe Cricket Club, seen here posing before a game at Budleigh Salterton. The following players have been identified: Peter Burch, Les Rolls, Chris Hookway, Graham Ferris, Peter Southall, Gerald Norton and Mike Ebdon.

Below we have the smiling members of the Marpool Primary School football team of 1979.

Front row: Stephen Gilbert, Shaun McNalty, Michael Hart, Graham Moore, and Tony Buckle.

Back row: Ian Thomas, Shane Avon, Saul Goodwin, William Davis, Peter Gilbert, and Caleb Goodwin.

Following the traditions and standards set by previous landlords was no easy task, but Claude and Elsie West became legends at the Holly Tree. He became the longest-serving licensed victualler in the district, while Mrs West – Elsie to the regulars – ably helped her husband behind the scenes.

Right, Fred Newport is shown presenting the cup to the winning team captains, Gabby Goodwin and Jamie Harris, at the Marpool County Primary Sports Day in 1977.

Below, we see a celebration of a very different kind – the end of the Second World War. Those that have been recognised at this victory party in 1945 include Geoff Marsden, Ron Coles, Mabel Pannell, Harold, Maud, Hilary and Maurice Southwell, Harold Burch, Marion Franks, Sid White, Sam Bowerman, Mrs Edwards and Mrs MacLean with Howard and Malcolm at the very back. Also recognisable are Mr and Mrs Coles with Pauline.

'Keeping up a tradition' is how one could describe the efforts of Tom Newton and Tom Mingo, shown here in the 1970s. Over the years pigeon lofts were a familiar sight in Withycombe; in the pigeon-racing world, both these men were known and respected well outside the parish boundaries. All these trophies were won in the West of England Continental Amalgamation competition, which was against 51 clubs from Devon, Cornwall and Somerset. The large tray and cup were won in a race of 545 miles from Hano in Germany.

The photograph at bottom right is much older and shows Mary and Neil Shapley with their dad, John, of Bystock Villas, Withycombe. He was President of the Exmouth Overseas Racing Pigeon Club, which had been founded in 1931. Other committee members from the village at that time included H. Cockeram, E. Lane and Son and Messrs Holmes and Jones.

The happy couple in the other photo are Alf and Liz Burch, shown celebrating their 60th Wedding Anniversary. They owned the general stores, which was by the Country House, and served the village well for many years.

The happy scene above comes from Brooklands Road. Those who have been positively identified include Mr Horsham, Mr Hastings, Mrs Bickley, Mrs Jack Burch, Mrs Frank Coles and Mike Coles, Mrs Coles (from the shop), Cecil Mothersole, Mrs Fred Lock, John Smith, Mr Coles, Mrs Mothersole, Miss Hastings, Mr Long, Mrs Selway, Mrs Long, Peter Burch, Brian Tozer, Christine Burch and Fred Burch.

Below is another VE Day celebration. Included in this picture, taken at the top of Masey Road, are Mr and Mrs Tew, with their daughters, Vera and Barbara.

In this 1957 group at Withycombe Raleigh Primary School we have Eric Evans, Chris Tate, John Tapscott, Marcus Bennet, Graham Dalley, Mike Maddley, Dave Hitchcock, John Tozer, Pam Franks, Jean Bird, Pat Bontoff, Barbara Tew, Susan Hurrell, Brenda Brain, Jane Strudwick, P. Sparks, Jenny Nunn, Ann Clarke, Edward Burch, Brian Jeffries, Andrew Pearson, Anne Sedgemore and John Fowler.

These amateur thespians shown below were made up of parents and staff at Marpool School in 1977.

This was the scene in 1993 when the old bakehouse, which had supplied generations of village families, was finally beaten by the violent storm. Pictured here is the village postmaster Tony Rait with his granddaughter, Lucy Charlotte Rait.

Below, the picture was taken not very long ago, and shows the original Withycombe Post Office in all its glory, shortly before its closure in 2003. The old bakery can be seen to the left.

In 1910 the Old Vicarage was made redundant with the new Vicarage moving to Brookhayes. It has changed hands several times. In 1920 Col H. Spackman came to Withycombe and made it his spacious home. Shortly afterwards he became Chief Officer of the Exmouth Fire Brigade, and was also a Commander of the Order of St John Ambulance Brigade. In 1937 it was all change again, when the Old Vicarage was bought by Miss Webster, the Headmistress of the new Senior Girls' Council School.

Two houses occupied the site of what is now the Nutbrook and Burnside housing estate; these were called, unsurprisingly, Nutbrook and Burnside. The Stanley family had created a Hotel at Burnside; Nutbrook was once the home of Philip Foale Rowsell, CBE, JP (1865–1946). He was

originally employed as manager for a firm which later became Holman, Ham & Co., manufacturing and retail chemists. He rose to the position of Managing Director. He was also a former President of the Pharmaceutical Society of Great Britain.

He took a keen interest in all Withycombe affairs, particularly in the Rugby Football Club, of which his son, Donald Rowsell, was Captain. A fluent speaker, in the General Election of 1929 he fought the Totnes Division as a Liberal, polling heavily and taking second place in a three-cornered contest. Soon after, he resigned his candidature. His grounds at Nutbrook were often open to the public in the summer, especially for fêtes and garden parties in connection with Withycombe Methodist Church.

Below was the sorry scene when hundreds of local people witnessed the destruction of the beautiful Monterey pine tree that had graced the grounds of Burnside; it had been a fine specimen and a village landmark. Burnside can be seen to the left of the tree, whilst on the right is Nutbrook. There will surely come a time, very soon, when both of these fine former buildings will be remembered only as road names.

Stoke Lyne was built in the 1870s as a holiday home for an Oxfordshire family; it was named after a village between Banbury and Bicester, where the family lived. As the head of the family did not enjoy going on holiday, his family had this house built as a replica of their own home to appease him. Unfortunately, it was demolished in 1995, despite attempts to save it. English Heritage suggested that it did not have sufficient 'architectural merit' to warrant it being listed. It was once owned by Miss Pinkney, a sister of Mrs Chichester of Marpool Hall. Miss Pinkney, despite her name, was said to be 'the Lady in Grey', reputed to haunt the upper floors of the house. In its latter years, the building was owned by the Exeter Health Authority, who provided accommodation here for children with learning disabilities.

Shown below, Knappe Cross is situated on the outskirts of Withycombe. Over the years it has served many uses: from 1940 to 1945, the building was an orphanage, the resident children attending lessons at the village school; it was later used as a convalescent home for Post Office workers. After becoming a hotel for a while, the house is currently a private nursing home. The picture shows the house some years ago, but the building and extensive grounds have changed very little, even today.

It is possible that Bassett's Park, shown above, was an extension of an earlier miller's or bailiff's cottage, a property developed and extended by Charles Wheaton. In the 1852/53 *Strangers Guide to Exmouth*, it was described in very lavish terms and said to be "situated in a picturesque and romantic Vale." In 1866 Bassett's Park was bought by Mr Otto (Ortho) Cooke, who changed the name to Withycombe House. In 1881 it was occupied by his son, Francis. However, records reveal that by 1889 it was owned by Mr John Stoole Tapper. The house is now described as a farmhouse.

The small photo to the right shows Jack Burch inspecting some of the handiwork of his father's business, which had provided this drain cover at Bystock Lodge.

Featured below, Bystock, like the Church of St John in the Wilderness, has seen many changes over the years, but they have both survived. However, the Bystock Estate has seen land sold for development. Now, with Dinan Way passing through the old Estate grounds, the question remains: will it eventually destroy the beautiful Wotton Valley?

We return to the heart of the village for our final two pictures in this volume. They are a reminder that change takes place not just over a period of years, but almost day by day. Above was the view looking down the road from the Country House pub. The former Recreation Room can be seen in the distance. Also in view are three houses with slate roofs and Oak Cottages, four thatched properties that had long gardens leading down to the road. On the other side of the road, Burch's Grocery shop has since been converted back into a private dwelling. The end thatched cottage was demolished, and the next cottage thus became semi-detached. The cottage at the other end of this row now has a slate roof; before the houses below were demolished, it was largely hidden from the road. Its entry, through a 'drangway', can be seen opposite the lamppost. Now, with pavements on both side of the road, it can be instantly recognised as the main entry into the Withycombe Primary Church School.

If you look closely at the houses in the picture below, you will notice that they are of different design: the first two, with the elaborate white brickwork, were called Elizabeth Cottages; the three beyond were known as Field View Cottages. Brickyard Cottages and Shortlands Cottages lay just around the corner. Who knows? Perhaps we may just take you around that bend, on a further pictorial journey around our lovely village of Withycombe Raleigh...